What People Are Saying About
Life with a Capital L

"The Christian church's first theologian, second-century Irenaeus, coined what remains the most accurate and penetrating definition of a Christian: 'The glory of God is man fully alive.' Matt Heard has taken that brief sentence and expanded it into this marvelous book, telling by story and observation, and using vigorous language (there is not a dull sentence in what he writes), to get us to embrace what has been given to us."

—EUGENE H. PETERSON, translator of *The Message*

"Matt Heard is a fresh new voice with a literally life-changing message. *Life with a Capital L* is a call to each of us to embrace our own humanity —just as God does. Here's a book that will deepen your walk with God and elevate your life to the level of Life."

—MARK BATTERSON, author of *The Grave Robber* and *All In*

"This is Praise with a capital P for *Life with a Capital L*. 'What does it mean to be alive?' and 'What does it mean to be human?' are two of the most important questions any human being can ask. They are questions that all Christians share with all of humanity. Matt Heard reflects on them with a warmth and honesty that will be welcomed by all who ask the questions."

—JOHN ORTBERG, author of *The Life You've Always Wanted*

"For years, I've treasured St. Irenaeus's words, 'The glory of God is man fully alive.' The quote rests on a shelf above my computer, and hardly a day goes by that I don't ask God to help me live out that enigmatic statement. Well, I now have a book to guide me. My friend, Matt Heard, writes winsomely and compellingly, answering that quiet aching so many people have—yes, even Christians—that there must be more to life. Trust me, the book you hold in your hands will awaken in you a deep desire to be all that God intended. I highly recommend *Life with a Capital L*!"

—JONI EARECKSON TADA, Joni and Friends International Disability Center

"The problem of pain may be one of the greatest challenges to faith in God, but the problem of pleasure can be more precarious. Disappointment in pleasure gives rise to emptiness, and sometimes not just for a moment but for life. Yet God created us for a purpose, and as Matt Heard writes, for so much more than we often recognize. Matt challenges us to look deeper into the mirror and to God who knows us fully and loves us intimately. *Life with a Capital L* is rich in encouragement, illustration, scriptural insight, and pastoral wisdom, and offers readers fresh insight and lasting hope."

—RAVI ZACHARIAS, author and speaker

"I know Matt Heard to be a thoughtful, humble follower of Christ. Those qualities are evident in *Life with a Capital L*. This book is a clear and powerful call to rediscover the depth and breadth of Life as God intended—to embrace the longing we all have to really Live as humans made in God's image."

—JIM DALY, president of Focus on the Family

"Matt goes to the heart of our need for Jesus. He makes us hope for heaven in a way that marks the everyday. He's a pastor, a leader, and a friend, and none of that is lost in these words."

—JENNIE ALLEN, author of *Restless* and founder of IF: Gathering

"Your world can be full of color, adventure, and discovery—Life with a capital L. Let Matt guide you on a journey to your full humanity—empowered, equipped, and inspired by the One who created you to live abundantly. Read this book and get ready to come alive in new ways!"

—LEE STROBEL, best-selling author of *The Case for Christ*
and professor at Houston Baptist University

"Matt Heard's new book is a deep well of resource for the soul. In *Life with a Capital L,* we have an invaluable resource to live the abundant Life of God, a map toward cultural life around us, and a blessing to re-humanize our world. Matt's approach toward beauty grows my heart as an artist and nourishes my creativity. His stories stir within me a deeper longing to create, love, and worship—with passion—our Savior-artist who pours grace into my heart."

—Mako Fujimura, artist, author, and culture-care catalyst

"This is what it's all about. Literally. Unless God's people understand what's in this book, we cannot be God's people. It's that important. Please read this book and rejoice that Matt Heard has written it!"

—Eric Metaxas, *New York Times* best-selling author of *Bonhoeffer: Pastor, Martyr, Prophet, Spy* and *Miracles: What They Are, Why They Happen, and How They Can Change Your Life*

"Matt Heard is a master storyteller, and peeking through all his stories is the Life Giver. I was struck by the intellectual depth of this book, but even more I was embraced by the personal Savior revealing himself through its stories. This book helped me see God not just in its pages but in my everyday experiences. Matt Heard ushers me into the greater Life."

—Dr. Joel C. Hunter, senior pastor of Northland, A Church Distributed

"An essential part of the gospel is often missed by Christians and left untold by churches: Christ didn't come to save us from our humanity but to return us to it! Matt Heard has skillfully preached and taught this for years, and now he skillfully articulates this truth through this book. Like me, I suspect readers will find themselves asking *What if? What if this is actually true?* and find their imaginations running wild with the Good News."

—John Stonestreet, speaker and fellow at Chuck Colson Center for Christian Worldview

"Life is a journey more than a destination. Matt Heard demonstrates and exemplifies this as one who seeks to be fully alive and longs for any who are interested to join him in that journey. This book is charged with all the stimulus and struggle that authentic human life must engage. Matt's artful portrait of Life is honest and hopeful, assured of God's love in Jesus Christ, but never glib or reductionist. This book awakens our thirst for Life as the real thing and nothing less."

—MARK LABBERTON, president of Fuller Theological Seminary

"Part Francis Schaeffer, part Max Lucado, and part Rick Steves, *Life with a Capital L* is one of those rare books that is both a page-turner and yet deeply contemplative. Matt Heard dives heart-first into Jesus's promise of a full Life and shows through biblical insight and hard-won experience how this promise is alive and well and meant for each of us. Matt's joyful engagement with art, music, food, conversation, travel, the Bible…and LIFE gives hope that God is actively restoring our humanity. Reading *Life with a Capital L* was a highlight of my year."

—JEFF MYERS, PhD, president of Summit Ministries

"*Life with a Capital L* will breathe new energy, new excitement, and new purpose into the life you are living. This is a challenge to all of us to go full tilt, be all in, and make it our ambition to embrace the fullness of what Life can and should be in relationship with Jesus. Being fully alive and fully human means we experience the eternal now. I'm fired up after reading this book!"

—BRAD LOMENICK, former president and key visionary of Catalyst, and author of *The Catalyst Leader*

"This book is Uplifting with a capital U. In it, Matt Heard pours out wise pastoral insights on being fully human."

—DON SWEETING, president of Reformed Theological Seminary in Orlando

"Many Christians have never considered that *abundant life* actually means becoming more human, not less. God's image lived out through us means we get to experience the fullness of what it means to be human, and to a skeptical world, that's Good News!"

—GABE LYONS, author of *The Next Christians*

"Matt Heard does not want to say something new but something old, only in a new, fresh way. And that he does well. Matt tells just the right story at just the right time. He writes with a pastor's heart and experience. He has read good books and learned from the masters. And he writes in a winsome, accessible style. His point is clear, compelling, and significant: we long for real Life, real Life can be ours, and real Life is available in Jesus Christ. This truth never grows old. Matt Heard knows this in his soul. This book is not simply about Life with a capital L. It actually conveys that Life."

—GERALD L. SITTSER, author of *A Grace Disguised,*
    A Grace Revealed, and *Water from a Deep Well,*
    and theology teacher at Whitworth University

"Loved Matt Heard's book on Life. I read it in one night and believe he squeezed the life out of the title. It's accented well with great personal stories; some of my all-time favorite quotes from Kierkegaard, Eliot, Pascal, and 'Babette's Feast'; and liberal use of appropriate Scripture. This book is the package."

—PEB JACKSON, Jackson Consulting Group

PARTICIPANT'S GUIDE

life
with a capital

life

with a capital

EMBRACING
YOUR
GOD-GIVEN
HUMANITY

matt heard

MULTNOMAH
BOOKS

Life with a Capital L Participant's Guide
Published by Multnomah Books
12265 Oracle Boulevard, Suite 200
Colorado Springs, Colorado 80921

All Scripture quotations are taken from the Holy Bible, New International Version®, NIV®. Copyright © 1973, 1978, 1984 by Biblica Inc.™ Used by permission of Zondervan. All rights reserved worldwide. www.zondervan.com.

Details in some anecdotes and stories have been changed to protect the identities of the persons involved.

Trade Paperback ISBN 978-1-60142-685-7
eBook ISBN 978-1-60142-686-4

Copyright © 2015 by Matt Heard

Cover design by Kristopher K. Orr; cover image by Mmdi, Getty Images

Published in association with the literary agency of Alive Communications Inc., 7680 Goddard Street, Suite 200, Colorado Springs, Colorado 80920, www.alivecommunications.com.

All rights reserved. No part of this book may be reproduced or transmitted in any form or by any means, electronic or mechanical, including photocopying and recording, or by any information storage and retrieval system, without permission in writing from the publisher.

Published in the United States by WaterBrook Multnomah, an imprint of the Crown Publishing Group, a division of Penguin Random House LLC, New York.

Multnomah and its mountain colophon are registered trademarks of Penguin Random House LLC.

The Cataloging-in-Publication Data is on file with the Library of Congress.

2015—First Edition

147028622

contents

Welcome 1

How to Use This Participant's Guide 3

Session 1. Realize Life While You Live It 7

Session 2. Recognize What You're Longing For 13

Session 3. Live Free .21

Session 4. Fight for Your Heart 29

Session 5. Savor the Beauty 35

Session 6. Turn Off the Dark 43

Session 7. Live the Great Story 49

Session 8. Bow Down Daily 57

Session 9. Be a Conduit of God's Love 65

Session 10. Seize the Life from Your Days 71

Session 11. Steward Your Pain 77

Session 12. Remember Your Destiny 85

Facilitator's Helps 93

My Resolutions for Life 95

Welcome

Everyone experiences ordinary heart-beating, lung-breathing life. Some are able to add to that existence some enjoyable relationships, a satisfying career, and maybe a level of financial success. Some will even add a bit of religiosity or spirituality to their repertoire. But not everyone experiences what I call Life with a capital L.

It's a way of doing life that can be present in every nook and cranny of our days—from heartbreaks to hobbies, client meetings to birthday celebrations, dinner parties to soup kitchens, funerals to vacations. From enduring an illness to enjoying concert tickets in the front row.

This is the kind of Life that Jesus meant when he said, "I have come that they may have life, and have it to the full" (John 10:10).

Fully alive. Fully human. So many of us are hungering for a gospel that's for human beings, not just spiritual beings. A gospel that brings us to Life in a fulfilling, God-glorifying way. Doesn't that resonate with what you're longing for?

When I wrote *Life with a Capital L: Embracing Your God-Given Humanity,* I did so with a conviction that it really needed to be more

than just a collection of words for people to read; it needed to be an experience. That's why I am excited to offer you this *Life with a Capital L
Participant's Guide.* As you participate in a group that is working through
these pages, you will engage in an experience together where you grow in
the Life that God always meant for you—a Life that, deep down, you
have always wanted. Through the introductory videos on the *Life with a
Capital L* DVD, I will come alongside you as a guide and encourager in
the journey.

Life with a capital L is best experienced in community—to enjoy it
to the full is to give it away to others. I'm excited for the ways you and
your group are about to explore and taste Life together.

To join the online conversation around Life with a Capital L, go to
Facebook.com/LifeWithACapitalLBook and LifeWithACapitalL.com.

How to Use This Participant's Guide

This participant's guide is designed to help you get more out of the book *Life with a Capital L* than you could get merely by reading it. Along with the related DVD, the participant's guide will serve as a helpful companion as you journey through the book.

The guide divides *Life with a Capital L* into twelve sessions. You can use it in a twelve-week, six-week, or four-week study, depending on the needs of your group.

6-Week Option	4-Week Option
Week 1: *Combine sessions 1 & 2*	Week 1: *Combine sessions 1 & 2*
Week 2: *Combine sessions 3 & 4*	Week 2: *Combine sessions 3 & 4*
Week 3: *Combine sessions 5 & 6*	Week 3: *Choose two of the Life experiences. For example, focus on session 5 (Beauty) and session 7 (Story)*
Week 4: *Combine sessions 7 & 8*	
Week 5: *Combine sessions 9 & 10*	Week 4: *Choose two more of the remaining Life experiences*
Week 6: *Combine sessions 11 & 12*	

You'll need a group leader. This person doesn't have to be a teacher but rather a facilitator of discussion. If you are the group leader, check out the "Facilitator's Helps" section at the back of this book for tips and suggestions you can use.

Let's look at what you can expect in the pages ahead.

The Group Session

Each of the twelve sessions follows the same format for journeying through these steps:

 Warm-Up Question. This is a question to get the conversation rolling and help you start thinking about how the chapter's theme relates to your own life.

 Video Reaction. Here is your chance to discuss what you see and hear on the introductory video that relates to the session.

 Word Study. Read and discuss the Scripture passage to make sure you're approaching the session topic with biblical illumination.

 Going Deeper. This is a box with some additional Scripture passages you may wish to read and consider during the group time or in your personal study.

 Group Discussion. These are conversation starters to help you discuss how to apply what you've learned in the book chapters and video. You can use all of the suggestions and questions or pick a few that will be best for your group.

 Closing Prayer. Finish your time talking with the Life-Giver. Ask God in the coming days to reinforce two or three key ideas and applications that have arisen from the group's discussion.

After the Session

After the material for the group session is a special section for individual use. It consists of reflection topics, Scripture meditation and prayer, and a unique commitment statement that you can use to create new habits for living Life with a capital L. At some point—soon after participating in the group session—use these elements during a quiet time alone with God.

Realize Life While You Live It

*Based on Chapters 1 and 2 of **Life with a Capital L***

Are we realizing life while we live it? Are we fully tasting what it means to be human? Too often, as the years pass, we become sleepy about the significance of our journey as human beings.

This opening session is intended to jolt you awake and send you into a new trajectory where you begin to unpack what it means to experience Life in the midst of living. To experience the dignity of the calling that's been embedded in your soul since the day you were born. To humbly relish the significance of who you are as a person created by God in his image. To acknowledge the longings God has placed within you as a human being. To embrace your full God-given humanity.

Many of us equate our humanity with our sinful nature and try to squelch it. But our humanity is not our sinful nature; rather it is the image of God in us. So we ought to be celebrating it! Under God's leadership, we should be seeking to live out our humanity more, not less.

The time to start really Living is now.

⬤ Warm-Up Question

1. As you think back on the way you have been conducting your life recently, how have you been just *doing* the activities of life and not really *living*? What might you have missed as a result?

⬤ Video Reaction

Watch video 1 on the *Life with a Capital L* DVD, taking notes as you wish:

> *Emily's penetrating question: Does anyone realize life while they live it?*

> *Being jolted awake*

> *Embracing our full humanity and true abundance*

> *How spirituality should enhance our humanity*

> *Jesus as not only the Way and the Truth but also the Life*

> *Our longings and what they reveal about us*

- How would you summarize what I conveyed in the video?

- Did any insights strike you as particularly intriguing or relevant to your own journey? Why?

Word Study

Read John 10:1–18, a teaching of Jesus that uses shepherding imagery.

2. What does Jesus (the gate and the good shepherd) do for his people (the sheep)?

3. Referring to verse 10, what do you think Jesus means by his declaration "I have come that they may have life, and have it to the full"?

Going Deeper

For further insight about realizing life while you live it:

- Genesis 1:27
- Psalm 8:4-8
- Psalm 139:14
- Ecclesiastes 3:10-11
- John 14:6
- 1 Corinthians 6:19-20
- Colossians 3:9-10
- 1 Peter 1:18

🫂 Group Discussion

4. Why do you think people so often fail to realize their life as they are living it? Is it due to personality, experiences, circumstances, pressures, fear, or what?

5. How do you think God feels about it when we are "sleeping" through our life?

6. Think about this last week. If you had lived each day fully awake to the significance of your human journey, how different would those days have looked?

7. In the past, have you tended to think of your humanity as a bad thing instead of a good thing? Where did you get that notion? How has it influenced you?

8. How can becoming more spiritually healthy enhance your humanity? How can your humanity reveal and enrich your spirituality?

9. How would your life change if you, with more regularity, humbly and gratefully embraced the reality that you and the people around you are God's image bearers?

10. In the book and the video, I convey the idea that a starting place for embracing our humanity is paying attention to the longings deep within our soul—the "eternity in our hearts." What are some unfulfilled or unaddressed longings inside you? Under God's leadership, how might they serve as a compass toward him and the Life he wants you to start living?

 ## Closing Prayer

Conclude your group interaction with a time in which volunteers pray out loud for God to help them fulfill their longing to embrace the abundant Life Christ offers.

❧ ❧ ❧

After the Session

For a quiet time between you and God.

Personal Reflection

Complete these sentences:

> One thing I appreciate about being created in God's image is . . .

> Despite all the good things in my life, what I still ache for is . . .

> One way I separate my spirituality from my humanity is . . .

Meditation and Prayer

Read and carefully meditate on the following declaration that Jesus made, and afterward talk with him about it.

> I have come that they may have life, and have it to the full.
> (John 10:10)

My Resolution

Use this resolution—as a springboard for prayer, reflection, and action—every day for as long as you need. (For a copy of this resolution that you can cut out and use, go to "My Resolutions for Life" on page 95.)

I resolve to realize life while I'm living it.

I will humbly and passionately embrace the significance of my own existence while also viewing and treating those around me as human beings created in the image of God.

I will engage with my humanity as a gift from God and will become more attentive to my longings, letting them lead me to a posture of deeper reliance on and intimacy with Christ—in both the spiritual and physical realms of my journey.

Recognize What You're Longing For

*Based on Chapters 3 and 4 of **Life with a Capital L***

We all have longings. But few of us make the effort to discern what those longings are and how they impact the way we spend our days and lives. On our journey toward Life with a capital L and full humanity, going deeper with our longings *and* with the gospel is vital.

It's important to understand that there's a difference between pursuits and longings (for example, we may be pursuing a career, but what we're longing for is significance). Our pursuits can be something good (from marriage to a hobby) or rebellious before God (from stealing to slander). And our core longings are rooted in the way God originally wired us when we were created in his image.

Sometimes our pursuits are mismatches for our longings. Accumulating wealth won't be able to provide the shalom our soul yearns for. If we're lonely, porn isn't going to help. So we need to look beneath our pursuits and identify our deeper longings, then think about what can actually address and satisfy those longings.

At the deepest level, what we all ultimately long for (even though many of us may not fully understand it) is eternal life—a deeper intimacy with God and a fuller experience of who he created us to be. Eternal life is as much about a quality of life as it is the duration of such a life. It's not just about *how long* we live but about *how* we live. It's Life with a capital L.

Only the pursuit of an intimate relationship with Jesus can satisfy our ultimate human longing to experience his Life in all the realms of our human journey.

Warm-Up Question

1. Would you describe yourself as a person who is filled with yearning—someone who has a deep longing for something more or something different out of life? Or are you content and satisfied with things just as they are? Explain.

Video Reaction

Watch video 2 on the *Life with a Capital L* DVD, taking notes as you wish:

Matt irritating a French waiter

How what we are going after in our lives is often very different from what we actually need

The difference between pursuits and longings . . . and the mismatch

What the woman at the well was really longing for

"Eternal life" as a qualitative phrase, not just a quantitative one—it's not just a synonym for heaven

The danger of missing the core of the gospel

- How would you summarize what I conveyed in the video?

- Did any insights strike you as particularly intriguing or relevant to your own journey? Why?

Word Study

Read John 4:1–18, the first half of the story of Jesus and the woman at the well. (We'll look at the second half in session 8.)

2. What deep longings do you think the woman kept futilely trying to satisfy in marriage after marriage and man after man?

Read Jeremiah 2:13, where the prophet talked about living water long
before Jesus did.

3. How is that passage relevant to Christ's offering of living water
   to the woman? What do you think he meant by his offer?

 Going Deeper

For further insight about recognizing
what you're longing for:
- Psalm 63:1
- Ecclesiastes 2:11
- John 5:24
- John 17:3
- John 20:31
- Romans 5:17
- 1 John 5:12

Group Discussion

4. Do you agree with this statement: "A superficial engagement
   with our longings will lead to a superficial engagement with the
   gospel"? Why or why not? During this season of your life, in
   which arena are you tending to stay more on the surface: your
   longings or the gospel?

5. At our core, we all have deep longings for things such as
   significance, intimacy, security, wholeness, goodness, truth,

beauty, freedom, shalom, resolution, destiny… What are some of your pursuits (for example, career, marriage, hobby)? What are the underlying longings that might be driving them? Are any of your pursuits inadequately suited to fulfill the longing(s) behind it?

6. Rooted underneath our deep longings is our ultimate longing: eternal life. In chapter 4 of *Life with a Capital L,* I describe eternal life this way: "To lovingly, submissively, vibrantly relate with God in such a way that it awakens my heart. Addresses my longings. Deepens my relationships. Permeates my work. Triggers my laughter. Authenticates my tears. Directs my journey. Fulfills my days. Restores my humanity." What part of that description resonates most with your yearnings? Why?

7. What could happen in your daily routine and journey if you started viewing eternal life as more than just a synonym for heaven—rather as a fulfilled longing that is to be experienced now as well as when you get to heaven?

8. Some church environments teach us to pursue Christ for a religious experience. Christ says to pursue him out of our ultimate longing for eternal life (a.k.a. "living water," Life

with a capital L) and, as a result, a fuller humanity. How will those two paths of pursuing him look different?

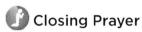 ## Closing Prayer

Start with a time of silent prayer in which group members can have some honest confession and conversation with God about their various pursuits and corresponding longings. Then finish with one person asking God to help everyone in the group to clarify their longings and align their pursuits with Christ's love, care, and provision for them.

❧ ❧ ❧

After the Session

For a quiet time between you and God.

Personal Reflection

Complete these sentences:

> If I am going to stop living in the shallows and go deeper with my longings, then I must . . .

> If I am going to bring my pursuits into line with my longings, then I had better . . .

> I will pursue God for an eternal quality of life by . . .

Meditation and Prayer
Read and carefully meditate on the following statement from Jesus and afterward talk with him about it.

> Everyone who drinks this water will be thirsty again, but whoever drinks the water I give him will never thirst. Indeed, the water I give him will become in him a spring of water welling up to eternal life. (John 4:13–14)

My Resolution
Use this resolution—as a springboard for prayer, reflection, and action— every day for as long as you need:

I resolve to recognize what I'm ultimately longing for.

I will go deeper in my understanding of both my longings and the gospel, discerning which longings are motivating my various pursuits.

I will cease compartmentalizing my relationship with Christ from the rest of my life and will acknowledge that my ultimate longing—in all my pursuits—is for him and his gift of eternal Life, which I can begin to experience now.

Live Free

Based on Chapters 5 and 6 of **Life with a Capital L**

Freedom to fully experience our lives as images of God is one of our core longings. But to Live in freedom, we must first taste grace.

When we practice a legalistic religiosity, we move away from grace and distance ourselves from freedom—and Life. When we grimly strive to do what we think will earn God's favor, we can easily miss out on the joy and beauty that God lavishes on us freely, simply as an act of grace. Instead of being hemmed in by man-made rules, he wants us to be free to Live.

Our freedom is experienced in the midst of Life-giving obedience that we practice in response to the grace and love that God has lavished on us through Jesus. Instead of opting for a counterfeit freedom where we do whatever we want, we instead let him lead us into Life with a capital L. It is then that we can enjoy the simple gift of embracing our God-given humanity on a daily basis.

Warm-Up Question

1. What does the grace of God mean to you?

Video Reaction

Watch video 3 on the *Life with a Capital L* DVD, taking notes as you wish:

A daily meal of grace

"Babette's Feast"

How the more legalistically religious we are, the less we experience grace

God lavishly blessing us with the Life of Christ

The parable of the prison cell

The difference between being free and living free

- How would you summarize what I conveyed in the video?

- Did any insights strike you as particularly intriguing or relevant to your own journey? Why?

 ## Word Study

Read Ephesians 1:6–8 and 2:1–10 (two passages about grace).

2. According to these passages, what does God's grace save us *from*? What does it save us *to*? How do these truths compare with your actual experience of grace?

Read Romans 8:1–4 (a passage about freedom).

3. According to these verses, what kind of freedom do we enjoy because of Christ?

 ## Going Deeper

For further insight about living free:
- Matthew 19:17
- Romans 5:17
- 2 Corinthians 3:17-18
- Ephesians 3:20
- 1 Peter 5:5

🎮 Group Discussion

4. In chapter 5 of *Life with a Capital L*, I talk about people taking a detour into religiosity, trying to earn God's favor by doing all the right things. When you've taken this detour, what were the implications of trying to perform for God?

5. What do you think and feel when you hear the word *lavish* (Ephesians 1:8) used to describe the way God demonstrates grace to you?

6. Tell about the time when you first confessed your sin and received Christ into your life (if you have indeed taken that step). What role has admitting your sin and your need for grace played in your life since then?

7. How does the counterfeit freedom of doing whatever we want differ from the true freedom that comes through obedience to God?

8. How does Life-giving obedience differ from Life-stealing religiosity?

9. How does obedience enable you to experience more abundant Life?

10. Here's a quote from chapter 6: "The freedom I have in Christ is the liberation to experience my humanity to the full, integrating both my spiritual as well as my physical realm—from relationships to vocation to emotions to finances to cultural impact to creativity to recreation." In what areas of life do you desire to experience freedom and more fully embrace your humanity?

Closing Prayer

Take turns thanking God for his lavish grace through Christ and asking his help to receive and Live in this grace on a daily basis.

❧ ❧ ❧

After the Session

For a quiet time between you and God.

Personal Reflection

Complete these sentences:

> I have chosen religion over relationship with God when I have . . .

In my life, bondage has looked like . . .

I will seek freedom and a fuller humanity through God's grace by . . .

Meditation and Prayer

Read and carefully meditate on the following verses from two letters by Paul, and afterward talk with God about them.

> Because of his great love for us, God, who is rich in mercy, made us alive with Christ even when we were dead in transgressions—it is by grace you have been saved. (Ephesians 2:4–5)

> There is now no condemnation for those who are in Christ Jesus, because through Christ Jesus the law of the Spirit of life set me free from the law of sin and death. (Romans 8:1–2)

If you're not yet a follower of Christ, this could be a prime time for you to take the step of receiving God's grace and entering the realm of Life. If so, here's a prayer you can pray as you transfer your trust to Christ for your salvation and restoration:

> Jesus, I acknowledge my need for you and the Life you alone can provide. I ask you to set me free from my spiritual prison cell that has hampered my ability to experience my full humanity. I confess my sin and my need for grace and accept your saving

work on the cross on my behalf. I submit to you as my Lord and Savior and receive your acceptance, forgiveness, freedom, and leadership. And I welcome your Life into my life so I may abundantly Live my days under your design. Amen!

If you prayed this prayer, welcome to Life!

My Resolution

Use this resolution—as a springboard for prayer, reflection, and action—every day for as long as you need:

I resolve to Live free.

I will taste God's extravagant grace and step out of my unlocked spiritual prison cell.

I will let my spiritual freedom fuel my freedom to engage with the whole spectrum of my journey as a human being, experiencing Christ's Life in all of my life.

Fight for Your Heart

*Based on Chapter 7 of **Life with a Capital L***

O ur heart is the core of our being. When we learn to live from the heart is when we begin to engage deeply with our own humanity and live with passion. Our heart is the launching pad of Life with a capital L.

A lot of people think the heart is just about emotions. Actually, the heart includes our emotions, but it is much more than our emotions.

The heart really serves as the hub of our humanity. Imagine three spokes on a wheel. One spoke is emotions, another is mind, and the third is will. The heart brings all three into complementary movement with each other. That's when our humanity moves to full throttle.

If we focus on just one of those areas, we'll get out of kilter and be excessively emotional, overly cerebral, or exceedingly impulsive.

If we're just *emotional* people, we'll engage with our feelings regarding situations we encounter but possibly miss the truth behind the situation.

If we're just *mind* people, we'll observe the facts of events and circumstances but miss their significance.

If we're just *willful* people, we'll have a lot of action, but we'll be on autopilot and won't really reflect on why we're doing what we're doing.

We need a fully alive and engaged heart to realize Life while we live it.

 ## Warm-Up Question

1. Imagine asking some of your closest friends, "Do I approach my life more with my mind as a thinker, with my emotions as a feeler, or with my will as a doer?" How do you think they would describe you?

 ## Video Reaction

Watch video 4 on the *Life with a Capital L* DVD, taking notes as you wish:

How the heart is often ignored and left flapping in the wind

FFYH and FWYH

The heart as the hub, coordinating thoughts, emotions, and actions

The heart like the needle of a record player, enabling us to experience what's going on in the grooves of our journey

Category 1, 2, 3, and 4 people

- How would you summarize what I conveyed in the video?

- Did any insights strike you as particularly intriguing or relevant to your own journey? Why?

Word Study

Read Proverbs 4:20–27, focusing especially on verse 23.

2. The biblical word translated "heart" in Proverbs 4:23 refers to the controlling core of our humanity, encompassing our mind, emotions, and will. With this definition in mind, what do you think it means to "guard your heart"?

3. Why is it so important that we guard our heart "above all else"?

Going Deeper

For further insight about fighting for your heart:

- Ecclesiastes 3:11
- Isaiah 61:1
- Ezekiel 36:26; 37:4-5
- Matthew 15:8-9
- Mark 12:30
- Romans 10:10

Group Discussion

4. Many of us didn't grow up in environments that taught us to live with heart. Why do you think that is the case?

5. How have you seen people become unbalanced—in their spirituality as well as their humanity—by being too focused on thinking, too focused on feeling, or too focused on acting? Why do you think they got off kilter? What were the consequences?

6. During this season of your journey, which aspect of your heart—mind, emotions, or will—might be more neglected than the others? What can you do to bring your heart back into balance?

7. In chapter 7, I wrote, "Fight for your heart and fight with your heart. Live your days thinking clearly, feeling deeply, and acting intentionally." What can you do to better fight *for* your heart? To fight *with* your heart? To live with passion?

8. How could restoring your heart to its proper role—engaging your heart more with your entire journey—lead you to a fuller humanity and enjoyment of God's grace and Life?

Closing Prayer

Pray together as a group for God to help members bring every aspect of their hearts into full operation so they can fully engage in Life with a capital L.

❧   ❧   ❧

After the Session

For a quiet time between you and God.

Personal Reflection

Complete these sentences:

I will think more clearly by . . .

I will feel more deeply by . . .

I will act more intentionally by . . .

The area of my life where I need to live with more passion is . . .

Meditation and Prayer

Read and carefully meditate on the following proverb, and afterward talk with God about it.

> Above all else, guard your heart,
>   for it is the wellspring of life. (Proverbs 4:23)

My Resolution

Use this resolution—as a springboard for prayer, reflection, and action—every day for as long as you need:

I resolve to fight for my heart.

I will experience the significance of my journey by engaging my renewed heart in every arena of my life—the highs and the lows, the broken and the beautiful.

I will live each day with passion by thinking wisely, feeling deeply, and acting intentionally in the presence of God.

Savor the Beauty

*Based on Chapter 8 of **Life with a Capital L***

As we learn to live Life with a capital L, our hearts are going to expand. And as that happens, we'll pay more attention to beauty—and be nourished by it.

I'm not talking about superficial, pretty, sentimental, or entertaining beauty. Instead, by "beauty," I'm referring to that which beckons us at a deep level regarding the privilege we have of being human. These are holy moments—sometimes lasting only a few seconds—when we say, "Wow, God, I get to be a part of a life in which I'm enjoying this beauty that I'm seeing or hearing or feeling! Thank you."

Too often, however, we use beautiful things, not to expand our appreciation of being human, but to deaden the pain of being in a fallen world. Used this way, beauty becomes a distraction rather than an enhancement to our journey.

Life with a capital L invites us to a place where we're authentically engaging with that which is beautiful. In the process, we experience the privilege of being human. Even further, we connect with a Creator who is the source of both beauty and life . . . and Life. Because, in the end, all beauty we see is just a fragment of the Whole: our beautiful God.

Seen this way, savoring beauty is a privilege, an opportunity, and a spiritual discipline.

 ## Warm-Up Question

1. What was something you saw or heard or experienced recently that made you say, "That's beautiful"? How did it impact you at the heart level, affecting the way you thought, felt, or needed to act?

 ## Video Reaction

Watch video 5 on the *Life with a Capital L* DVD, taking notes as you wish:

Saving minutes but missing moments

How beauty isn't just for distracting us from the pain of being in a fallen world

Using beauty to expand our appreciation of being human

How beauty connects us with a beautiful God

Letting fragments lead me to the Whole

Saying "That's beautiful" and then saying "God, you're beautiful"

- How would you summarize what I conveyed in the video?

- Did any insights strike you as particularly intriguing or relevant to your own journey? Why?

🔲 Word Study

Read Philippians 4:4–9, an often-quoted passage where Paul told us what to focus our minds and hearts on.

2. How would a person actually go about dwelling on things that have the admirable qualities Paul mentioned? In other words, what might it look like in a person's daily life to put Philippians 4:8 into action?

Read John 14:6, another familiar verse.

3. We can easily view Jesus as the Way and the Truth but overlook our engagement with his Life. What can go wrong if Christians

focus on goodness (morality) and/or truth (biblical orthodoxy) while neglecting beauty?

Going Deeper

For further insight about savoring the beauty:

- Psalm 19:1-4
- Psalm 27:4
- Psalm 50:2
- Psalm 84:1
- Ecclesiastes 3:11
- Isaiah 52:7
- Matthew 13:15
- 1 Corinthians 13:9-12

Group Discussion

4. What are some beautiful things that move you the most? (For example, types of art, such as music, painting, or dancing; natural scenery; human athleticism.)

5. Give an example of a way in which you have approached beauty in a less than ideal way, perhaps treating it as mere entertainment or as a distraction from the problems of life.

6. At other times, how have you felt beauty enrich, expand, and deepen you?

7. In chapter 8 of *Life with a Capital L,* I say, "All true beauty bears the fingerprint of God." Describe a way in which you have caught a glimpse of the Author of beauty via some kind of earthly beauty.

8. Do you agree with this notion: "If we appreciate fragments of beauty only for themselves, not as part of the whole of God's beauty, that diminishes our experience of the beauty." Why or why not?

9. How has your experience of beauty influenced your relationship with God? How has your relationship with God influenced your experience of beauty?

10. How open and responsive to beauty would you say you are generally? To the extent that you tend to neglect beauty, what's inhibiting you? What could you do to savor more of the beauty in the world?

Closing Prayer

As a group, give thanks to God for the gifts of beauty he offers us. Praise him for his own surpassing beauty.

෴ ෴ ෴

After the Session

For a quiet time between you and God.

Personal Reflection

Complete these sentences:

> If I'm honest with myself, I have to admit that I sometimes neglect or misuse the world's beauty by . . .

> I'd like to be moved to worship God whenever I encounter beauty in the form of . . .

> If I want to start noticing and appreciating the beauty around me more, the first steps I would take would be to . . .

Meditation and Prayer

Read and carefully meditate on the following verse from Philippians, and afterward talk with God about it.

> Whatever is true, whatever is noble, whatever is right, whatever is pure, whatever is lovely, whatever is admirable—if anything is excellent or praiseworthy—think about such things.
> (Philippians 4:8)

My Resolution

Use this resolution—as a springboard for prayer, reflection, and action— every day for as long as you need:

I resolve to savor beauty.

As I pay attention to beauty in a wide variety of forms, I will declare, "That's beautiful," more often and more deeply, appreciating both the beauty itself and its ultimate creator, God.

Furthermore, I will be an instrument of beauty in my relationships and my culture.

Turn Off the Dark

*Based on Chapter 9 of **Life with a Capital L***

Light and life go together. It's true in nature. It's true as well in our journeys as human beings. Life with a capital L depends on the amount of illumination we have.

That's why Jesus said, "I am the light of the world. Whoever follows me will never walk in darkness, but will have the light of life" (John 8:12). Jesus himself is our light.

But he went on to say, "If you hold to my teaching, you are really my disciples. Then you will know the truth, and the truth will set you free" (verses 31–32). So obedience leads to freedom via the truth.

That brings us to another source of light: the Scriptures. The psalmist prayed, "Your word is a lamp to my feet and a light for my path" (Psalm 119:105). If we will obey him, God's Word will lead us on the path of Life.

Some people think the Bible is just a handbook for a certain religious club. They think it has limited applicability, at best pertaining only to spiritual things. But I want to suggest it is really something more. Much more.

What if we were to rely on the Bible, not just to live a correct *Christian* life, but to live a fulfilling *human* life under God's leadership?

Warm-Up Question

1. What role does the Bible play in your life?

Video Reaction

Watch video 6 on the *Life with a Capital L* DVD, taking notes as you wish:

> *Scuba-diving at night without an underwater light*

> *Feeling lost in the journey of being a human*

> *Jesus as the light of the world and the Bible as light for our journey*

> *The Bible as more than a rule book, doctrinal handbook, or devotional tool*

> *God's Word as a guide not only for a Christian life but for a human life*

- How would you summarize what I conveyed in the video?

- Did any insights strike you as particularly intriguing or relevant to your own journey? Why?

 ## Word Study

Read John 8:12, 31–32. These passages show Jesus clarifying who he is and how his followers can know freedom through obedience to his teaching (and by extension, through obedience to all the divinely inspired words of Scripture).

2. Referring to John 8:12, what do you think "light" and "darkness" refer to?

3. With John 8:31–32 in mind, how have you found obedience to God's teaching to be liberating?

Going Deeper

For further insight about turning off the dark:

- Psalm 16:11   - Proverbs 16:25
- Psalm 56:13   - Isaiah 9:2
- Psalm 89:15   - John 1:4
- Psalm 119:105

🫧 Group Discussion

4. What do you think most people in our society think about the Bible?

5. When you were growing up, how did you see the Bible being used?

6. Why, at times, do we tend to resist scriptural instruction and not choose God's light and illumination for our journey? What are some of the most prominent reasons?

7. What are the different ways you learn from the Bible (sermons, classes, books, group Bible studies, personal devotions, and so on)? What's most helpful to you?

8. I talk about viewing the Bible not only as handbook for a Christianity that's correct but for a humanity that's fulfilling— not just about how to live a Christian life but how to live a human life before God. How could that perspective change the way you read and study the Bible?

9. What can you do differently to access the Bible's wisdom as a source of illumination for your journey through life?

Closing Prayer

Pray for diligence to seek out God's guidance in his Word, for humility to receive it, for wisdom to apply it, and for courage to follow it.

~ ~ ~

After the Session

For a quiet time between you and God.

Personal Reflection

Complete these sentences:

> One way in which my attitude toward the Bible isn't as faithful as it could be is . . .

> I would get more out of Scripture if I were more disciplined to . . .

> If I were to approach the Bible less as a means to understand facts and more to get instruction on how to live, that would mean . . .

Meditation and Prayer

Read and meditate on the following words from the lips of Jesus, and afterward talk with him about it.

> If you hold to my teaching, you are really my disciples. Then you will know the truth, and the truth will set you free. (John 8:31–32)

My Resolution

Use this resolution—as a springboard for prayer, reflection, and action—
every day for as long as you need:

I resolve to turn off the dark in my journey.

I will treat the Bible as a manual for my
full humanity and not just my spirituality,
as a source of illumination about how to
Live and not just what to believe.

I will Live out of the Word by studying,
listening to, meditating on, memorizing,
and applying it.

Live the Great Story

*Based on Chapter 10 of **Life with a Capital L***

For us to engage with our humanity, to live Life with a capital L, it's important that we understand the bigger story that our own personal story is a part of. If we don't, the monotonous day-in, day-out pace of merely surviving to play and playing to survive, with no larger sense of purpose, will deaden us before we ever get to the grave.

God's Word tells us the bigger story of what he is doing in history. What is it all about? It's about God restoring the fullness of his glory to his creation.

That phrase—*God's glory*—tends to make our eyes glaze over. It seems archaic, and we've heard it many times. It doesn't seem relevant to the way we do our careers, our recreation, our family life, and the rest of normal living.

But that perception could not be further from the truth. God's glory, and the bigger story of restoration it's a part of, has everything to do with the daily activities and concerns of our lives. Because we find our ultimate purpose within God's glory. Like all the rest of creation, we are meant to contribute to the expansion of God's glory. As Paul said, "Whatever you do, do it all for the glory of God" (1 Corinthians 10:31).

And what *is* God's glory? It is his *enoughness* for all of creation and for you and me. To glorify God means that, whatever we're doing, we're to revel in the sufficiency, the majesty, and the enoughness of God. It means to engage daily with his purpose of restoring all things to reflect his glory.

 ## Warm-Up Question

1. How have you struggled with knowing and pursuing the purpose of your life?

 ## Video Reaction

Watch video 7 on the *Life with a Capital L* DVD, taking notes as you wish:

> *The hobbits returning—transformed—to the Green Dragon tavern*

> *The importance of understanding the larger context of what we're doing*

> *A great blessing of the gospel—being able to grasp the larger story*

God's glory as his enoughness for all creation, including me

How the story of God's glory serves as a map or big picture

The essence of our empty rebelliousness as falling short of the glory of God

- How would you summarize what I conveyed in the video?

- Did any insights strike you as particularly intriguing or relevant to your own journey? Why?

Word Study

Read Habakkuk 2:12–14, a vision of the restoration of God's glory to his creation that supersedes the most strenuous efforts human societies could put forth.

2. What are some of the grand designs that human beings pursue only to see them fall flat when they conflict with the purposes of God?

3. What is the promise of verse 14? How do you think it is being fulfilled?

Going Deeper

For further insight about living the story:

- Romans 6:4
- 1 Corinthians 10:31
- 2 Corinthians 3:17–18
- 2 Corinthians 4:6
- Colossians 1:27
- Hebrews 2:9–10

Group Discussion

4. Think of a time you have experienced a sense of monotony or meaninglessness in your life. Describe it.

5. How would you say your personal story is connected with the grand story of what God is doing in history? How does this connection make you feel?

6. To you, what does the glory of God mean and how does your heart engage with it?

7. What is it about *who God is* that is glorious? What is it about *what God is doing in history* that is glorious?

8. If we aren't particularly excited about the glory of God, why might that be? What can we do to capture a vision for why God's glory should be paramount to us?

9. Is it hard for you to surrender the starring role of your story to God, taking a minor (though significant) role for yourself? Or is it easy? Explain.

10. Read the following from chapter 10 in *Life with a Capital L:* "Embracing that I am part of the larger story of God's glory will change the way I live out my humanity. It will change the way I eat, drink, do the dishes, and mow the lawn. It will change the way I pursue my vocation and enjoy my vacations. It will change the way I love, laugh, and cry." Give some specific examples of how you intend for God's story of restoring his glory to change some of your everyday pursuits.

🟠 Closing Prayer

Have volunteers offer prayers of their own, thanking God for the opportunity of having their lives upgraded with meaning as they bring their personal stories into alignment with God's great story.

≈ ≈ ≈

After the Session

For a quiet time between you and God.

Personal Reflection

Complete these sentences:

> What I really feel about my life story becoming a part of God's greater story is . . .

> I am in awe of God whenever I think of . . .

> In light of God's glory, I will approach the rest of my day differently by . . .

Meditation and Prayer

Read and meditate on the following poetic-prophetic image from Habakkuk, and afterward talk with God about it.

> The earth will be filled with the knowledge of the glory
>   of the Lord
>   as the waters cover the sea. (Habakkuk 2:14)

My Resolution

Use this resolution—as a springboard for prayer, reflection, and action—every day for as long as you need:

I resolve to Live the great story.

I will realize, in both my awareness and
my behavior, that the story in which I'm
playing a part—at work, at home, with
friends, in recreation, or wherever I am—
is not merely about me but is primarily
about God and the restoration of his
glory.

Whether I am eating or drinking or
whatever I'm doing, I will to do it all
for the glory of God, embracing and
reflecting his enoughness for me and
all creation.

Session 8

Bow Down Daily

*Based on Chapter 11 of **Life with a Capital L***

We're all wired to worship. You and I have never come across a human being who didn't worship someone or something.

We may believe in God or not believe in God. Regardless, *everyone* worships; it's not just church people. We all elevate various things to become objects of worship by devoting our time, our energy, our resources, our hopes, and our dreams to them.

The issue is not *whether* we'll worship but *who* or *what* we'll worship. In fact, Christ's invitation to live Life with a capital L is a summons for my everyday worship to be restored toward the right object. And when our worship is aimed in the right direction, it becomes a Life-giving catalyst toward a fulfilled humanity.

God seeks our ultimate worship—he wants us to elevate him above every other idolatrous god and potential object of worship. It's not because he is insecure or has ego issues, but because he knows that when we worship him we'll fulfill the original purpose we were made for and experience the Life that only he can provide.

So whom are we worshiping?

Are we worshiping with our whole lives?

 Warm-Up Question

1. Do you feel a craving for worship? What does your worship look like?

Video Reaction

Watch video 8 on the *Life with a Capital L* DVD, taking notes as you wish:

> *Matt pursuing an elk while simultaneously being pursued by a mountain lion*

> *The woman at the well being led to see the connections among her longings, pursuits, and worship*

> *Everyone being a worshiper*

> *Particular pursuits that we elevate by devotion of our time, resources, and energy*

In the midst of our pursuits, God pursuing us . . . for worship

Saying to the pursuing God, "Thank you for your grace and living water"

- How would you summarize what I conveyed in the video?

- Did any insights strike you as particularly intriguing or relevant to your own journey? Why?

🔖 Word Study

Read John 4:19–26. This is the second half of the story of the woman at the well, which we started looking at in session 2.

2. Although the woman may have just been trying to change the subject when she brought up worship, how was the topic of worship relevant in her life?

3. What does it mean to "worship in spirit and truth"?

Going Deeper

For further insight about bowing down daily:

- Psalm 34:3
- Psalm 37:4
- Jeremiah 2:11–13
- Habakkuk 3:17–18
- Romans 1:25
- Ephesians 1:11–12
- 1 Peter 2:9

Group Discussion

4. John Calvin wrote that we humans are "idol factories," continually turning things in our lives into objects of worship. What are some of the potential go-to idols in your life and with other people you know?

5. In chapter 11 of *Life with a Capital L,* I propose, "Worship [of God] is central to being fulfilled as a human being." Do you agree? Why or why not?

6. How can we make worship not just something we do at church but something we do with our whole life, acknowledging God's

worth through our work, our recreation, our relationships, and every other part of what we do? Give examples.

7. How are our longings related to what and who we worship?

8. In times of difficulty and confusion, we can lean toward desiring resolution so much that we worship answers more than we worship God. What would it involve to counter such a tendency?

9. If someone were to follow you around for a day, what evidence would he or she see that you are a worshiper of God?

10. What changes could you make, starting today, to worship God *only* and to worship him *wholly*?

🅕 Closing Prayer

As a group, commit to worshiping God alone. Ask his help to reorient your everyday lives around worshiping him in all you do.

❧ ❧ ❧

After the Session

For a quiet time between you and God.

Personal Reflection

Complete these sentences:

> I need to confess to God that I have created an idol of . . .

> Some ways I could expand the worship of God in my life include . . .

> An area of my life where I need to trust God and continue to worship him, even though I am distressed or confused, is . . .

Meditation and Prayer

Read and meditate on the following statement Jesus made, and afterward talk with him about it.

> A time is coming and has now come when the true worshipers will worship the Father in spirit and truth, for they are the kind of worshipers the Father seeks. (John 4:23)

My Resolution

Use this resolution—as a springboard for prayer, reflection, and action— every day for as long as you need:

I resolve to bow down daily.

In the midst of my pursuits—whether
public or private, working or playing—
I will acknowledge that God is pursuing
me for my ultimate worship.

I will then consciously do my life in his
presence, celebrating and responding
to the supreme worth of who he is and
what he does.

In all areas of my life, including the
mysteries behind my unanswered
questions, I will embrace the truth that
his Life is what will ultimately satisfy me.

Be a Conduit
of God's Love

*Based on Chapter 12 of **Life with a Capital L***

Loving relationships—with God and other people—are a powerful catalyst of Life with a capital L. God has poured his love into each of our lives. Will we let that love flow through us into the lives of people around us? Or will we hoard it? Will we be a pipe or a bucket?

The truth is, when we stop loving the people around us, we stop experiencing the love of God. (He continues to love us, but we stop *experiencing* it.) On the other hand, when we take the love that God has given us and turn around and give it to the people around us, we experience God's love as it was meant to be experienced.

John 3:16 says, "God so loved the world that he gave his one and only Son, that whoever believes in him shall not perish but have eternal life." God loves us to Life. As we've continued to see throughout our study, that "eternal life" is not just future tense. And a primary way we can experience that Life right now is by receiving God's love and giving it away.

So as we grow in our grasp of God's love for us, as we become con-duits of that love to the people around us, and as we also let those other people love us, that's when we experience the beautiful flow of Life with a capital L.

 ## Warm-Up Question

1. Tell about a time when someone did something self-sacrificially loving for you. How did it make you feel?

Video Reaction

Watch video 9 on the *Life with a Capital L* DVD, taking notes as you wish:

Life either thwarted or enjoyed in the context of relationships

The realm of Life as a place of love

The difference between a bucket and a pipe

John 3:16 and God loving us to Life

The absolute, unconditional love of God

Experiencing God's love as we pass it on to others instead of hoarding it

- How would you summarize what I conveyed in the video?

- Did any insights strike you as particularly intriguing or relevant to your own journey? Why?

Word Study

Read 1 John 3:11–18, where the apostle John talked about the connection between Life and love.

2. Looking at verse 14, why do you think John singled out love as both a litmus test for having received Christ's Life and a primary determiner of whether we are experiencing that Life?

Going Deeper

For further insight about being a conduit of God's love:

- Psalm 67:1-2
- Isaiah 43:4
- Isaiah 54:10
- John 3:16
- John 13:34
- Romans 8:14-15
- Ephesians 3:18
- Ephesians 4:32—5:2
- 1 John 3:1
- 1 John 4:9-10

🎴 Group Discussion

3. What reasons do you have for believing that God loves you?

4. Lately, have you been more like a pipe (serving as a conduit of God's love to others) or a bucket (hoarding God's love)? Explain.

5. In chapter 12 of *Life with a Capital L,* I identified some common reasons for failing to pass on God's love to others:
    a. We're not experiencing God's love fully ourselves because we think it's a reward for performance instead of a free gift.
    b. We either smother people with our insecurity or cut ourselves off from them due to our woundedness.
    c. We're just plain selfish.

   Describe a way in which you have seen one of these motivations at work in cutting off the flow of love between people.

6. How can we experience Life with a capital L in the face of rejection or betrayal?

7. What are some practical ways we can share the love of God

with others, from close friends in need of care to oppressed strangers in need of justice and to others in between?

8. What can we expect to receive in return when we share God's love with others?

 ## Closing Prayer

In prayer, thank God for his unconditional love and seek his help in sharing that love freely with others.

❧ ❧ ❧

After the Session

For a quiet time between you and God.

Personal Reflection

Complete these sentences:

Recently, I wasn't as loving as I should have been when . . .

The reason I wasn't more loving on that occasion is . . .

I'm going to choose to share the love of God with others (being a pipe) by . . .

Meditation and Prayer

Read and meditate on the following verse from 1 John, and afterward talk with God about it.

> We know that we have passed from death to life, because we love our brothers. Anyone who does not love remains in death. (1 John 3:14)

My Resolution

Use this resolution—as a springboard for prayer, reflection, and action—every day for as long as you need:

I resolve to be a conduit of God's love.

I will Live as someone who is accepted and loved unconditionally by God and, as a result, will turn my attention toward others, pursue authentic Life-giving community, and act as a pipe instead of a bucket of his Life-giving love and grace.

Seize the Life from Your Days

*Based on Chapter 13 of **Life with a Capital L***

I call it life math: our lifetime is simply the sum of our individual days. Yet, too often, the way we spend our individual days is different than the way we want our overall life to turn out.

It's like grapes. If you mix a bunch of bad or low-quality grapes together, you're never going to be able to make great wine. Likewise, a bunch of ill-spent days added together are not going to result in a well-lived life.

A powerful way to ensure that we're practicing healthy life math is to number our days. To realize our days are not infinite and they will come to an end. We don't need to panic because our time on earth is finite. But we *do* need to be intentional about what we do with the time we have. That will counter a tragic tendency we have to continually procrastinate living, saying, "*Tomorrow* I'll get serious and really live Life."

Daily Life with a capital L will lead to a Lifetime with a capital L.

Yes, we've got to *carpe diem*—seize the day. But even more, we've got to seize the *Life* out of each day.

 ## Warm-Up Question

1. Do you ever have the feeling you're not really living but instead are more or less just putting in time until you really start to live, hopefully, sometime in the future? If so, tell about it.

 ## Video Reaction

Watch video 10 on the *Life with a Capital L* DVD, taking notes as you wish:

> *The difference between the ways that novice golfers and advanced golfers act on the practice range*

> *Numbering our days*

> *The human tendency to put off really living*

> *Life math*

> *Seizing the Life out of each day*

- How would you summarize what I conveyed in the video?

- Did any insights strike you as particularly intriguing or relevant to your own journey? Why?

Word Study

Read Ephesians 5:8–20, where Paul told his readers to wake up and start paying more attention to how they were living.

3. When you read Paul's words about making the most of every opportunity (verse 16), what is it in your own life that you think about?

4. What do the contrasts—living in light or darkness, with wisdom or foolishness, being intentional or careless—suggest to you about how to make the most of your time and opportunities?

Going Deeper

For further insight about seizing the Life from your days:

- Psalm 27:4
- Psalm 39:4
- Psalm 90:9–12
- Proverbs 13:14
- Ephesians 1:9–10
- 1 Timothy 6:12

🫂 Group Discussion

5. If you were to live out an average life expectancy, about how much time would you have left on this earth? Is your reaction to your life expectancy fear, a posture of ignoring your mortality, or a desire to make the most of the time you have left?

6. What's an example of a missed opportunity in your life that you regret? What is an example of an opportunity that you seized and that gives you satisfaction to look back on?

7. In chapter 13 of *Life with a Capital L*, I described the difference between two Greek words for time: *chronos* (the ordinary passage of time) and *kairos* (a significant moment that you either seize or lose). Do you have a *kairos* opportunity before you right now? If so, describe it.

8. If we wanted to distinguish between what is important in life and what is not, how would we go about the discernment process?

9. Is there something you've been doing that you need to stop doing because it fruitlessly drains too much precious time? Is there something you've been putting off that you ought to get to without further delay?

10. I talked about living in the "presence tense." What is an area of your life where you can resolve to be less distracted or careless and be more fully present?

Closing Prayer

Ask God to teach all of you to number your days and make the most of every opportunity he gives you.

✤ ✤ ✤

After the Session

For a quiet time between you and God.

Personal Reflection

Complete these sentences:

Today I will stop procrastinating about . . .

Today I will quit wasting my time with . . .

Today I will be courageous and seize the opportunity to . . .

Meditation and Prayer

Read and meditate on the following verses from Ephesians, and afterward talk with God about them.

Be very careful . . . how you live—not as unwise but as wise, making the most of every opportunity. (Ephesians 5:15–16)

My Resolution

Use this resolution—as a springboard for prayer, reflection, and action— every day for as long as you need:

I resolve to seize the Life from my days.

I will experience the Life that's present in each day instead of procrastinating my engagement with its *kairos* moments— both the beauty and the brokenness.

I resolve each day to take hold of the eternal Life to which I've been called and with which I've been gifted, living out my day as one who is fully present and desiring to intentionally taste the Life that is everywhere.

Steward Your Pain

*Based on Chapter 14 of **Life with a Capital L***

In our life journey, we enter new realms of maturity by passing through experiences that are often painful. Sometimes the pain comes from our own rebelliousness or knuckleheadedness. Sometimes it comes through the immaturity or sin of other people. Or maybe it's just a result of living in a fallen world. The bottom line is that the broken experience is there, it's painful, and yet it can serve as a gate that will lead us to a greater experience of Life.

We can't avoid painful difficulty. But we do have a choice regarding how we will respond to the gate before us. We've got two options.

First, when we encounter a gate of a broken experience—a painful situation—we can try to *escape* it by medicating ourselves or retreating from it. This may relieve us temporarily, but it also means we won't benefit from what the pain can teach us. We won't grow or move into the next arena of maturity. We will stagnate.

The second choice is to *engage* with the difficulty, to willingly walk through the gate. I don't mean that we masochistically seek out broken experiences. Instead, we accept unavoidable pain and learn what God can teach us through it. I call this the *stewardship* of pain. We accept it as something we are to make the most of and grow through.

Taking the first option—escape—leads to woundedness. Taking the second option—stewardship—leads us to brokenness, and that's a very different thing from woundedness. Wounds fester. Broken places heal and become stronger than before. Brokenness brings Life while woundedness stifles it.

The choice to relate with God in the midst of our pain, trusting him to redeem it, and grow through our broken experiences leads us to deeper Life with a capital L.

Warm-Up Question

1. Is there a particular broken experience—physical, emotional, spiritual, financial, or relational—you are struggling with right now? Describe it.

Video Reaction

Watch video 11 on the *Life with a Capital L* DVD, taking notes as you wish:

Fantine's song in Les Misérables

Approaching pain with a sense of stewardship

Pasture theology

Broken experiences serving as a gate into greater Life

The distinction between brokenness versus woundedness

Pliability versus resistance when we encounter broken experiences

- How would you summarize what I conveyed in the video?

- Did any insights strike you as particularly intriguing or relevant to your own journey? Why?

Word Study

Read James 1:2–8, a passage that puts the trials of life in a very different perspective than most of us are used to.

2. When have you seen testing lead to perseverance? When have you seen perseverance lead to spiritual maturity?

3. How close would you say you are to being thankful about what you are learning from the trials of your life?

Going Deeper

For further insight about stewarding your pain:

- Job 23:10
- Psalm 18:32–33
- Psalm 23:4–5
- Psalm 56:8
- Psalm 95:7–8
- Psalm 147:3–5
- Isaiah 42:2–3
- Isaiah 61:1–3
- John 5:5–6
- John 16:33
- Romans 8:28
- 1 Corinthians 13:12
- 2 Corinthians 4:8–10

Group Discussion

4. Describe a time in the past when you tried to escape from a painful experience, perhaps by pretending it wasn't real (using drugs or alcohol or busyness or entertainment to mask it) or otherwise trying to ignore or avoid it. How did your attempts to escape the experience help or hurt you in the long run?

5. What does it mean to engage with the pain in our lives? Give an example or two of what that might look like.

6. Tell about a time when you opened yourself up to what God wanted to teach you through a difficult situation and what you learned through it.

7. What makes painful gate experiences so useful in moving us on toward greater spiritual maturity and a fuller, more robust humanity?

8. What is an area of your life right now where God is calling you to engage with a broken experience? Are you welcoming or resisting this engagement? Why? What new wisdom or guidance might God have for you if you are willing to steward the pain?

Closing Prayer

Spend two minutes in silent prayer as group members pray for the grace to steward their broken experiences and mature through them for God's glory.

～ ～ ～

After the Session

For a quiet time between you and God.

Personal Reflection

Complete these sentences:

> The situation that hurts the most for me right now is . . .

> If I were to stop trying to merely escape from pain and start opening my heart to what God wants to teach me in the midst of it, I would . . .

> What I'm hoping God will do for me as a result of the broken experiences in my life is . . .

Meditation and Prayer

Read and meditate on the following verses from the book of James, and afterward talk with God about them.

> Consider it pure joy, my brothers, whenever you face trials of many kinds, because you know that the testing of your faith develops perseverance. Perseverance must finish its work so that you may be mature and complete, not lacking anything. (James 1:2–4)

My Resolution

Use this resolution—as a springboard for prayer, reflection, and action— every day for as long as you need:

I resolve to steward my pain.

I will make the most of my broken experiences by approaching each one with a pliable heart, seeing it as a maturing opportunity to taste more deeply the Life of Christ and the beauty of brokenness.

I will guard against bitterness and woundedness by embracing, with real hope, the truth that God can and will redeem beauty from whatever painful ashes I encounter in this broken world.

Remember Your Destiny

*Based on Chapter 15 of **Life with a Capital L***

To be fully human, to live Life with a capital L, means living a life of significance. And one of the biggest differences between significance and insignificance is having a sense of destiny—knowing we have purpose and are headed somewhere—and then living our life accordingly.

As followers of Jesus, we're headed toward the restoration of all things in the new heaven and new earth. We're headed toward that Great Day when God's glory will be restored completely to his creation. Remembering this on a daily basis can capitalize our Life.

When we're dealing with sickness, we can remember that one day we're going to get a new body that will know no illness or death.

When we're enjoying the beauty of the world, we can tell ourselves, "This creation is still fallen. Imagine what the new earth will be like!"

When we experience painful events, we can say, "It will not always be so. There will come a day when ashes will be turned to beauty."

When we need to obey a command of God, it can be a reminder of the time when we will stand before the judgment seat of Christ and be rewarded for seeking first God's kingdom.

Even our unfulfilled longings can remind us that we are not yet home.

People talk about being so heavenly minded that we're no earthly good. That's only a problem if we're using heaven as an escape. But biblically, heaven is not an escape; it's a goal. It's not a cop-out; it's our compass.

 ## Warm-Up Question

1. Do you think very often about dying and going to heaven? What does the hope of heaven mean for you?

 ## Video Reaction

Watch video 12 on the *Life with a Capital L* DVD, taking notes as you wish:

Living life backward

Being mindful about our mortality

Heaven as a solid hope based on the resurrection of Jesus

*Moments when we can engage with the hope of heaven—
sickness, creation, broken experiences, obedience, longings*

*The Life of heaven—immortal bodies, total freedom, pure
hearts, undiluted beauty, illumination by God, culminated
story, face-to-face worship, perfect love, healed brokenness, the
end of time*

"Now go Live"

- How would you summarize what I conveyed in the video?

- Did any insights strike you as particularly intriguing or relevant
  to your own journey? Why?

Word Study

Read 2 Corinthians 5:1–10, a very personal expression where we can al-
most hear the apostle Paul's groans of longing to live in a resurrected body
with Christ.

2. Unpack Paul's images in verses 1–5. What is the "tent"?
   What is the "eternal house"? What is meant by being
   "clothed"? What is meant by being "naked"? What does

it mean for "what is mortal" to be "swallowed up by life"? How is the Holy Spirit a "deposit"?

3. As you look at verses 6–10, what would you say was Paul's attitude toward our heavenly future? How did it influence him during his earthly life?

Going Deeper

For further insight about remembering your destiny:

- Romans 8:18–21
- 1 Corinthians 2:9
- 1 Corinthians 13:12
- 1 Corinthians 15:52–54
- 2 Timothy 1:10
- 2 Peter 3:13
- 1 John 3:2
- Revelation 21:1–4
- Revelation 22:1–5

Group Discussion

4. What things remind you that this world is not your ultimate home—and that heaven is instead?

5. What are you most looking forward to in heaven?

6. How does the prospect of heaven affect how you live your life right now? In what ways should it perhaps affect how you're living *more* than it already does?

7. How could you help others to have a hope of heaven and to experience Life with a capital L?

8. Of the ten experiences of Life with a capital L (in chapters 6–15 of the book), which one resonates most with you? Why?

9. How has your life changed since you began this study of *Life with a Capital L*? What would you like the rest of the members of the group to pray about for you as you begin to more deeply Live?

Closing Prayer

As this study comes to a close, consider standing as a group and giving thanks to God for how he has used you in one another's lives during these weeks, and pray for one another. Also thank him for the way he is graciously leading you into a Life of full humanity and abundance.

Now go Live.

≈ ≈ ≈

After the Session

For a quiet time between you and God

Personal Reflection

Complete these sentences:

> The part of my earthly life that I'm most looking forward to
> being done with after death is . . .

> What I'm longing for most about my future Life in heaven
> is . . .

> Because I have a glorious destiny to look forward to in the
> presence of God, today I will . . .

Meditation and Prayer

Read and meditate on the following passage from 2 Corinthians, and
afterward talk with God about it.

> We know that if the earthly tent we live in is destroyed, we have
> a building from God, an eternal house in heaven, not built by
> human hands. Meanwhile we groan, longing to be clothed with
> our heavenly dwelling, because when we are clothed, we will not
> be found naked. For while we are in this tent, we groan and are

burdened, because we do not wish to be unclothed but to be clothed with our heavenly dwelling, so that what is mortal may be swallowed up by life. (2 Corinthians 5:1–4)

My Resolution
Use this resolution—as a springboard for prayer, reflection, and action—every day for as long as you need:

I resolve to remember my destiny.

I will keep in mind that my ultimate redemption is graciously secured and that Christ will get me Home.

I will pay attention to today's "heaven moments"—whether physical aches, unfulfilled longings, encounters with beauty, broken experiences, or opportunities to obey—and will hope for the day when Life with a capital L will no longer be diluted by a fallen body and fallen world.

Facilitator's Helps

Being the facilitator of a group using the *Life with a Capital L Participant's Guide* is not difficult to do, but it is important. During your meeting times, it's mainly a process of keeping the discussion moving forward. Yet, if you do take on that role, it will give you the privilege of helping all the group members experience the fullness of Life that Jesus promised. Thank you for your willingness to serve them!

Tips for the Facilitator

- Think about how you might want to promote your *Life with a Capital L* discussion group. For example, do you want to schedule a presentation at your church? Make sure everyone who chooses to take part in the group has a copy of *Life with a Capital L* as well as a copy of this participant's guide. Gather phone numbers or e-mail addresses so you can communicate with the participants. Give them a reminder of when and where the first session is to be held.

- Each week before your group gets together, watch the video and work through the participant's guide session material on your own. Think through the key points—what they mean to you, what they might mean to your group members. Read the "Going Deeper" passages and perhaps read a Bible commentary on the "Word Study" passage. Pray for God to be at work in you and in your group.

- If you're going to have refreshments, arrange for someone to take care of that.
- Get to the group meeting location ahead of time to ensure you have everything you need. Test the video equipment with the DVD. Have some Bibles, pens, and notepaper on hand. Maybe you'd like a whiteboard too. Check to see that the seating, lighting, room temperature, and other components of the environment are suitable for a comfortable conversation.
- Welcome everyone who shows up. Introduce participants to each other if they're not already acquainted. Perhaps you'll want to have an icebreaker question ready at the beginning of at least the first session to help people feel more comfortable with each other.
- Either at the beginning of a session or at the end, you may choose to take personal prayer requests and lead the group in prayer for them.
- During the discussion time, ask the questions aloud for the group. If some participants seem as though they would like to say more but are feeling too shy, gently draw them out. If others are monopolizing the group's time, politely interrupt them and redirect the conversation. Feel free to add to, skip over, or adapt some of the questions in the participant's guide to personalize the discussion for your group. Keep watch over the progress of the conversation to make sure you can cover all the important points in the time you have available. Yet if it seems that God is doing something special in the group, by all means go with that, even if it means deviating from your original plan.
- Encourage group members to use the "After the Session" sections on their own at home.

My Resolutions for Life

Clip these resolutions and carry them with you—or place them in a location where you will see them often—and be reminded of the habits you desire to form in order to live Life with a capital L.

---

1. I resolve to realize life while I'm living it.

I will humbly and passionately embrace the significance of my own existence while also viewing and treating those around me as human beings created in the image of God.

I will engage with my humanity as a gift from God and will become more attentive to my longings, letting them lead me to a posture of deeper reliance on and intimacy with Christ—in both the spiritual and physical realms of my journey.

2. I resolve to recognize what I'm ultimately longing for.

I will go deeper in my understanding of both my longings and the gospel, discerning which longings are motivating my various pursuits.

I will cease compartmentalizing my relationship with Christ from the rest of my life and will acknowledge that my ultimate longing—in all my pursuits—is for him and his gift of eternal Life, which I can begin to experience now.

3. I resolve to Live free.

I will taste God's extravagant grace and step out of my unlocked spiritual prison cell.

I will let my spiritual freedom fuel my freedom to engage with the whole spectrum of my journey as a human being, experiencing Christ's Life in all of my life.

4. I resolve to fight for my heart.

I will experience the significance of my journey by engaging my renewed heart in every arena of my life— the highs and the lows, the broken and the beautiful.

I will live each day with passion by thinking wisely, feeling deeply, and acting intentionally in the presence of God.

5. I resolve to savor beauty.

As I pay attention to beauty in a wide variety of forms, I will declare, "That's beautiful," more often and more deeply, appreciating both the beauty itself and its ultimate creator, God.

Furthermore, I will be an instrument of beauty in my relationships and my culture.

6. I resolve to turn off the dark in my journey.

I will treat the Bible as a manual for my full humanity and not just my spirituality, as a source of illumination about how to Live and not just what to believe.

I will Live out of the Word by studying, listening to, meditating on, memorizing, and applying it.

7. I resolve to Live the great story.

I will realize, in both my awareness and my behavior, that the story in which I'm playing a part—at work, at home, with friends, in recreation, or wherever I am—is not merely about me but is primarily about God and the restoration of his glory.

Whether I am eating or drinking or whatever I'm doing, I will to do it all for the glory of God, embracing and reflecting his enoughness for me and all creation.

8. I resolve to bow down daily.

In the midst of my pursuits—whether public or private, working or playing—I will acknowledge that God is pursuing me for my ultimate worship.

I will then consciously do my life in his presence, celebrating and responding to the supreme worth of who he is and what he does.

In all areas of my life, including the mysteries behind my unanswered questions, I will embrace the truth that his Life is what will ultimately satisfy me.

9. I resolve to be a conduit of God's love.

I will Live as someone who is accepted and loved unconditionally by God and, as a result, will turn my attention toward others, pursue authentic, Life-giving community, and act as a pipe instead of a bucket of his Life-giving love and grace.

10. I resolve to seize the Life from my days.

I will experience the Life that's present in each day instead of procrastinating my engagement with its *kairos* moments—both the beauty and the brokenness.

I resolve each day to take hold of the eternal Life to which I've been called and with which I've been gifted, living out my day as one who is fully present and desiring to intentionally taste the Life that is everywhere.

11. I resolve to steward my pain.

I will make the most of my broken experiences by approaching each one with a pliable heart, seeing it as a maturing opportunity to taste more deeply the Life of Christ and the beauty of brokenness.

I will guard against bitterness and woundedness by embracing, with real hope, the truth that God can and will redeem beauty from whatever painful ashes I encounter in this broken world.

12. I resolve to remember my destiny.

I will keep in mind that my ultimate redemption is graciously secured and that Christ will get me home.

I will pay attention to today's heaven moments—whether physical aches, unfulfilled longings, encounters with beauty, broken experiences, or opportunities to obey— and will hope for the day when Life with a capital L will no longer be diluted by a fallen body and fallen world.

About the Author

Matt Heard lives in Colorado Springs with his wife, Arlene, where they have relished the privilege of raising three amazing sons—Andrew, Joel, and Stephen.

A speaker, writer, consultant, and Bible teacher, Matt has been involved in pastoral ministry and leadership for three decades. He is a graduate of Wheaton College and Reformed Theological Seminary and has pastored churches in Illinois, Michigan, and Colorado. Most recently he served as senior pastor of Woodmen Valley Chapel in Colorado Springs for twelve years. He has also been a leadership consultant and was the executive director of the Greater Orlando Leadership Foundation (now Lifework Leadership).

Matt enjoys skiing, fishing, and hunting in the Rocky Mountains. He appreciates great food, art, music, books, and movies. He's a sports nut, a passion that includes golf, scuba-diving, and being a diehard fan. He also loves to ride, either a horse or his Harley.

And whether standing in front of people with a microphone, in a trout stream with a fly rod, or serving a need in his city, he most of all loves exploring and experiencing Christ's ultimate gift, Life with a capital L, and inviting other people into the journey.

To find out more or to contact Matt, visit www.mattheard.org.

Printed in the United States
by Baker & Taylor Publisher Services